EVERYONE LOVES
NEW YORK

EVERYONE LOVES
NEW YORK

teNeues

INTRODUCTION

BY LESLIE JONATH

As F. Scott Fitzgerald once said, "New York had all the iridescence of the beginning of the world." Whether or not you were born in New York, the city is as much a state of mind as it is a geographical place. A city of limitless experiences, New York City has inspired art, artists, and art movements in an infinite number of styles and perspectives. And as Truman Capote once said, "I love New York, even though it isn't mine, the way something has to be, a tree or a street or a house, something, anyway, that belongs to me because I belong to it."

Everyone Loves New York features tributes to this world-renowned American city from artists around the world: from the spires of the Chrysler Building and expansive gardens of Central Park to the watchful lions gracing the entrance of The New York Public Library and the treasures of the Museum of Modern Art; from the graceful arches of the Brooklyn Bridge to the iconic Lady in bronze, the Statue of Liberty. Look carefully in the book and you will also discover the small pleasures of each neighborhood that make New York City so compelling: flowerboxes on a West Village townhouse, a sun-drenched day in Harlem, graphic street signs in Chinatown, the ubiquitous yellow taxicabs crowding the avenues, its ever-popular street food, and the great melting pot that is the New York subway experience. And you can't forget the city's archetypal citizens—New Yorkers—bike messengers to starry-eyed lovers to dog walkers and gallery goers, are all featured here.

New York has an ineffable quality of making one feel both included and excluded at the same time. Author and adopted New Yorker, Tom Wolfe, may have said it best: "Even if you have never lived in New York, once you arrive, you may feel that one belongs to New York instantly, one belongs to it as much in five minutes as in five years."

EINLEITUNG
VON LESLIE JONATH

Der Schriftsteller F. Scott Fitzgerald hat einmal gesagt: „New York schillerte in den Regenbogenfarben einer Welt am ersten Tag." Egal, ob man in New York geboren wurde oder nicht, die Stadt ist nicht nur ein geografischer Ort, sondern auch ein Geisteszustand. Als Metropole der unbegrenzten Möglichkeiten hat New York die Kunst, ihre Strömungen und Künstler zu unzähligen Stilen und Sichtweisen inspiriert. Und von Truman Capote stammt der Satz: „Ich liebe New York, obwohl es mir nicht gehört, so, wie mir etwas gehören muss, ein Baum oder eine Straße oder ein Haus, irgendetwas jedenfalls, das zu mir gehört, weil ich zu ihm gehöre."

Everyone Loves New York präsentiert eine Sammlung von Liebeserklärungen an diese weltberühmte amerikanische Großstadt von Künstlern aus aller Welt. Die Spitze des Chrysler Building und das weite Grün des Central Park werden ebenso gewürdigt wie die wachsamen Löwen, die das Portal der New York Public Library zieren oder die Schätze des Museum of Modern Art. Überall finden sich Zitate, wie etwa die anmutigen Spitzbögen der Brooklyn Bridge oder das bronzene Sinnbild Amerikas, die Freiheitsstatue. Sehen Sie genau hin, und Sie werden auch die kleinen Besonderheiten der einzelnen Stadtteile entdecken, die New York so unwiderstehlich machen: Blumenkästen an einem Townhouse im West Village, ein besonders sonniger Tag in Harlem, die Schriftzeichen auf den Straßenschildern in Chinatown, die allgegenwärtigen Yellow Cabs, die durch die Avenues drängen, die beliebten Straßenimbisse und der große Schmelztiegel namens New Yorker U-Bahn. Nicht zu vergessen die Archetypen des New Yorkers an sich, die alle in diesem Buch vertreten sind – vom Fahrradkurier bis zum verträumten Liebespaar, vom Hundeausführer bis zum Galeriebesucher.

New York sorgt auf unnachahmliche Weise dafür, dass man sich im selben Maße zugehörig wie ausgeschlossen fühlt. Der Schriftsteller und Wahl-New-Yorker Tom Wolfe hat es vielleicht am besten ausgedrückt: „Selbst wenn du nie in New York gelebt hast – sobald du ankommst, spürst du, dass du sofort zu New York gehörst, man gehört nach fünf Minuten genauso dazu wie nach fünf Jahren."

INTRODUCTION
PAR LESLIE JONATH

Comme l'a dit une fois F. Scott Fitzgerald, « New York a toute l'iridescence de la création du monde ». Que vous soyez né ou non à New York, la ville est autant un état d'esprit qu'un lieu géographique. Ville des expériences sans limites, New York a inspiré l'art, les artistes et les mouvements artistiques dans un nombre infini de styles et de perspectives. Et comme l'a dit une fois Truman Capote, « J'aime New York, même si ce n'est pas ma ville, il doit bien y avoir quelque chose, un arbre, une rue ou une maison, en tout cas quelque chose qui m'appartient à moi parce que moi j'en fais partie ».

Everyone Loves New York est un hommage à cette ville américaine mondialement réputée, par des artistes de toute la planète : de la flèche du Chrysler Building et les jardins immenses de Central Park aux lions vigilants ornant l'entrée de la bibliothèque publique de New York et les trésors du Musée d'art moderne ; des arcs élégants du pont de Brooklyn à l'iconique Dame de bronze, la Statue de la Liberté. Regardez attentivement et vous découvrirez aussi dans ce livre les petits plaisirs de chaque quartier qui rendent la ville de New York tellement fascinante : les boîtes à fleurs d'une maison mitoyenne de West Village, un jour inondé de soleil à Harlem, les pancartes des rues de Chinatown, les taxis jaunes omniprésents qui encombrent les avenues, la nourriture toujours populaire vendue dans la rue et ce grand melting pot que vous découvrez dans le métro de New York. Et impossible d'oublier l'archétype des citoyens, les New Yorkais, des messagers en vélo aux amoureux qui voient des étoiles, ceux qui promènent leur chien ou vont visiter les galeries, ils sont tous là.

New York a ce don ineffable de vous faire sentir à la fois inclus et exclu en même temps. Auteur et New Yorkais d'adoption, Tom Wolfe, l'a parfaitement dit : « Même si vous n'avez jamais vécu à New York, une fois arrivé, vous pouvez vous sentir immédiatement comme chez vous, vous êtes intégrés aussi bien en cinq minutes qu'en cinq ans ».

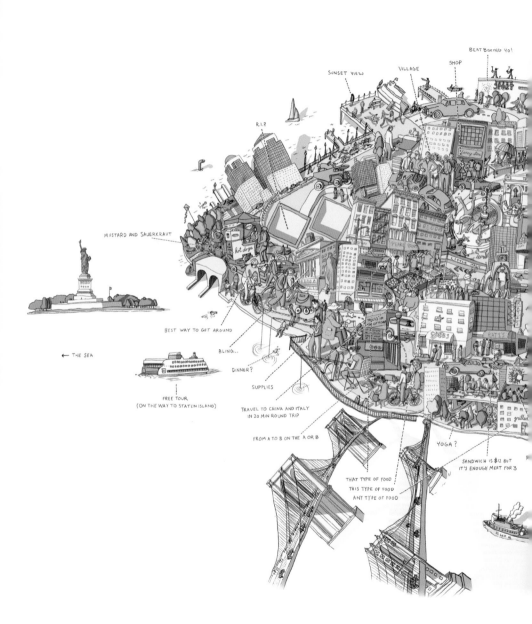

BEAT BOXING YO!

SUNSET VIEW

VILLAGE

SHOP

R.I.P.

MUSTARD AND SAUERKRAUT

hot dogs

KATZ'S

grilled

← THE SEA

BEST WAY TO GET AROUND

BLING...

DINNER?

SUPPLIES

FREE TOUR
(ON THE WAY TO STATEN ISLAND)

TRAVEL TO CHINA AND ITALY
IN 20 MIN ROUND TRIP

FROM A TO B ON THE A OR B

YOGA?

SANDWICH IS $12 BUT
IT'S ENOUGH MEAT FOR 3

THAT TYPE OF FOOD
THIS TYPE OF FOOD
ANY TYPE OF FOOD

I THINK I CAN

NORTH
(TO CANADA)
N

STATUE OF THAT GUY....

BOAT PARTIES

THE PRETTY ONE

THE TALL ONE

ART ART ART!

BROADWAY SHOWS

REAL NY'ERS
(IN A RUSH)

FARM FRESH

TOUR

THE BEST AND THE WORST

TANGO SUNDAY

ROLLER DISCO

FREE

CLASSICAL STUFF

STRAND BOOKS

PIZZA

EVERY ONE
IS DIFFERENT

GET HERE
GET THERE

BOYS IN BLUE

MIGHT SEE ANYTHING

MIGHT BE COOL,
MIGHT BE CRAZY

NEW ART

OLD ART

ANOTHER COMMUTER

AMERICAN ART

18 MILES OF BOOKS

AN AFTERNOON
EXPLORATION

LOOKING FOR
CONEY ISLAND

MY BIKE COMMUTE

25

27

THE SOLOMON R GUGGENHEIM MUSEUM

Stephen Wiltshire

Corbasson

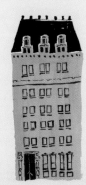

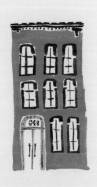

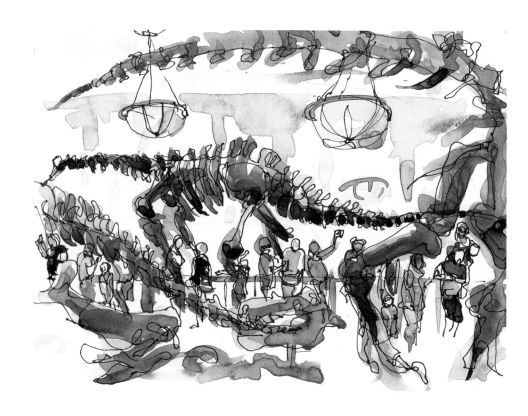

CENTRAL

53

61

michael sterings

Sarah M[?]Menemy

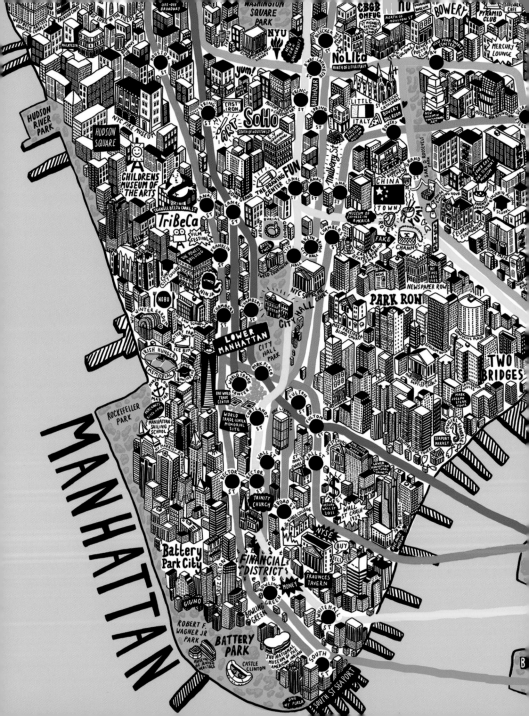

The TOURIST

These cyclists are most often seen riding rent-a-bikes, wearing fanny packs and stopping abruptly in the middles of bridges to take scenic photos. They are generally underexperienced and physically unfit for a demanding urban environment such as NYC.

The MESSENGER

This cyclist has no time for bullshit. There are long plastic tubes to be delivered to tall buildings. As highly evolved utilitarians who have a fearless and instinctual command of NYC traffic, they flow down Broadway like fish downstream. However, their cunning is too often the cause of their demise.

PEARL PAINT

508

www.pearlpaint.com

113

brooklyn.south street.china town.little italy.village

i♥nyc

the village.chelsea.east side.west side.central park.

ARTIST CREDITS

Cover:
Clare Caulfield

2
Barbara Macfarlane

4
Michael Mullan

9
Katie Daisy

10-11
Clare Caulfield

12
Laura Amiss

13
Laura Amiss

14
Tim Hopgood
www.timhopgood.com

15
Smiljana Coh

17
Benoit

18
Christopher Corr

20-21
Rebecca Stadtlander

23
Brenna Thummler

24-25
Leif Parsons

26
R. Nichols

27
SANDY M

28
Patricia van Essche

30-31
Kevin Woest

32
Stephen Wiltshire

34-35
Emily Isabella

37
Emily Isabella

38
Christopher Corr

39
Dominique Corbasson/ cwc.i.com.

40
R. Nichols

42
Sujean Rim

43
Danielle Kroll

44
Michael Storrings
Images from *New York in Four Seasons*
© 2014 by Michael Storrings.

45
Michael Storrings
Images from *New York in Four Seasons*
© 2014 by Michael Storrings.

46
Suhita Shirodkar

47
Suhita Shirodkar

48-49
Julia Rothman
Image from *Hello NY* © 2014 by
Julia Rothman. Used with permission
of Chronicle Books, San Francisco.

50
Marianna Coppo

51
Emma Block

52
Blanca Gómez

53
Ligang Luo

54
R. Nichols

55
Elizabeth Baddeley

56-57
Adam Corns

58
Dominique Corbasson/ cwc.i.com

59
Dominique Corbasson/ cwc.i.com

60-61
Violet Lemay
From the book *New York Baby*.
Art by Violet Lemay

62
Jorge Colombo

63
Jorge Colombo

65
Bil Donovan

66
Michael Storrings
Image exclusive to The Plaza Hotel

67
Dominique Corbasson / cwc.i.com

68-69
Luke Cloran

71
Carlo Stanga
Underground Gallery (2009)

72
Clare Caulfield

73
Strand Book Store

74-75
Suhita Shirodkar

76
Kendyll Hillegas

77
Bella Pilar

78-79
Veronica Lawlor

80
Brigette Barrager

83
Mark Ulriksen

84
Emma Block

85
Emma Block

86
Sarah McMenemy

87
Sarah McMenemy

88-89
Jenni Sparks

90
Kurt McRobert

91
Kurt McRobert

92-93
Emily Isabella

94
Anna Simmons

96-97
Rebecca Clarke

98
Jennifer Orkin Lewis | Courtesy of
Jennifer Nelson Artists.

99
Édith Carron

101
Annelise Capossela

102
Anna Higgie

103
Shari Blaukopf

LESLIE JONATH

Leslie Jonath is the author of numerous books including *Everyone Loves Paris*, *Postmark Paris*, *Bee & Me*, *At the Farmer's Market with Kids*, *The Dictionary of Extraordinary Animals*, and *Give Yourself a Gold Star* as well as the blog, *Feed Your People: Food to Gather Around*. In addition to writing books, she is also the founder of Connected Dots Media, a content packaging company that creates beautiful illustrated books and content on food, cooking, art and design, pop culture, and other odd and eclectic topics. www.connecteddotsmedia.com

Leslie Jonath hat zahlreiche Bücher verfasst, darunter *Everyone Loves Paris*, *Postmark Paris*, *Bee & Me*, *At the Farmer's Market with Kids*, *The Dictionary of Extraordinary Animals* und *Give Yourself a Gold Star*. Außerdem schreibt sie für den blog *Feed Your People: Food to Gather Around* und ist die Gründerin von Connected Dots Media, einem Unternehmen für Content Packaging, das schöne Bildbände und Inhalte zu den Themen Ernährung, Kochen, Kunst und Design, Popkultur sowie zu weiteren Sujets unterschiedlichster Art produziert. www.connecteddotsmedia.com

Leslie Jonath est l'auteur de nombreux livres dont, Cachet de la *Everyone Loves Paris*, *Postmark Paris*, *Bee & Me*, *At the Farmer's Market with Kids*, *The Dictionary of Extraordinary Animals* et *Give Yourself a Gold Star*, sans oublier le blog, blog *Feed Your People: Food to Gather Around*. Outre le fait d'écrire des livres, elle a également fondé Connected Dots Media, une entreprise de conditionnement qui crée de beaux livres illustrés et des contenus sur la nourriture, la cuisine, l'art et le design, la culture pop et d'autres sujets insolites et éclectiques. www.connecteddotsmedia.com

ACKNOWLEDGEMENTS

I would like to thank the incredible artists herein who graciously shared their art and love for New York. I would also like to extend a huge thanks to the wonderful people at teNeues Publishing, especially to art director Allison Stern, editor Carla Sakamoto, as well as to Audrey Barr and Harald Thieck, and to my amazing team: Jessica Goss, Katje Richstatter, and Miel Lappin.

DANKSAGUNG

Ich danke den wunderbaren Künstlern dieses Buches, die ihre Kunst und ihre Liebe zu New York mit uns geteilt haben. Mein großer Dank gilt auch den wunderbaren Menschen bei teNeues, insbesondere der Artdirektorin Allison Stern, der Redakteurin Carla Sakamoto sowie Audrey Barr und Harald Thieck, und nicht zuletzt meinem tollen Team: Jessica Goss, Katje Richstatter und Miel Lappin.

REMERCIEMENTS

Je tiens à remercier les artistes incroyables qui ont gracieusement partagé leur art et leur amour pour New York. Je voudrais aussi dire un grand merci aux gens merveilleux de teNeues Publishing et tout particulièrement à la directrice artistique, Allison Stern, la rédactrice, Carla Sakamoto, ainsi que Audrey Barr et Harald Thieck, et mon équipe extraordinaire : Jessica Goss, Katje Richstatter et Miel Lappin.

Everyone Loves Paris by Leslie Jonath
© 2015 Leslie Jonath. All rights reserved.

Text and concept by Leslie Jonath
Translations by:
Dr. Kurt Rehkopf (German)
Helen Solody-Wang (French)
Design by Allison Stern
Editorial coordination by Carla Sakamoto
Production by Dieter Haberzettl
Color separations by

Published by teNeues Publishing Group

teNeues Media GmbH + Co. KG
Am Selder 37, 47906 Kempen, Germany
Phone: +49-(0)2152-916-0
Fax: +49-(0)2152-916-111
e-mail: books@teneues.com

Press department: Andrea Rehn
Phone: +49-(0)2152-916-202
e-mail: arehn@teneues.com

teNeues Publishing Company
7 West 18th Street, New York, NY 10011, USA
Phone: +1-212-627-9090
Fax: +1-212-627-9511

teNeues Publishing UK Ltd.
12 Ferndene Road, London SE24 0AQ, UK
Phone: +44-(0)20-3542-8997

teNeues France S.A.R.L.
39, rue des Billets, 18250 Henrichemont, France
Phone: +33-(0)2-4826-9348
Fax: +33-(0)1-7072-3482

www.teneues.com

ISBN 978-3-8327-3259-2

Library of Congress Number: 2015940197

Printed in Czech Republic.

teNeues Publishing Group
Kempen
Berlin
London
Munich
New York
Paris

teNeues